MT. ACONCAGUA
ARGENTINA / HEIGHT: 22,840 FEET / 6,962 METERS

MT. DENALI
(MCKINLEY) - UNITED STATES (ALASKA)
HEIGHT: 20,310 FEET / 6,190 METERS

MT. ELBRUS
RUSSIA / HEIGHT: 18,510 FEET / 5,642 METERS

MT. EVEREST
NEPAL/TIBET
HEIGHT: 29,032 FEET / 8,849 METERS

MT. KILIMANJARO
TANZANIA / HEIGHT: 19,341 FEET / 5,895 METERS

THE SEVEN SUMMITS

These mountains represent the highest peaks on each of the seven continents. Climbing all seven is a major goal for mountaineers worldwide.

MT. KOSCIUSZKO
AUSTRALIA (MAINLAND)
HEIGHT: 7,310 FEET / 2,228 METERS

MT. VINSON
ANTARCTICA / HEIGHT: 16,050 FEET / 4,892 METERS

THE SEVEN SUMMITS

MOUNT EVEREST

HANK MUSOLF

CREATIVE EDUCATION • CREATIVE PAPERBACKS

Published by Creative Education and Creative Paperbacks
P.O. Box 227, Mankato, Minnesota 56002
Creative Education and Creative Paperbacks
are imprints of The Creative Company
www.thecreativecompany.us

Design by Graham Morgan
Art direction by Blue Design (www.bluedes.com)

Images by Alamy Stock Photo/Royal Geographical Society, 14–15; Associated Press, 38–39; Association Chantal Mauduit Namaste, 10; Dreamstime/Daniel Prudek, 25, Extezy, cover, 1, Grejak, 34, Pecorb, 1, Vac, 20, Wirestock, 22; Flickr/Frank Kehren, 35; Getty Images/AFP, 36, Boy_Anupong, 9, Express Newspapers, 16, Fred Ramage, 17, Gary Qian, 18, hadynyah, 24, imageBROKER/Johannes Pfatschbacher, 21, Jason Maehl, 32, jonpic, 27, NAMGYAL SHERPA, 40, 41, Nick Pedersen, 43, Robert Holmes, 26, Pexels/Marina Zvada, 45, Prabin Sunar, 2; Public Domain, 29; Unsplash/Parth Savani, 4–5; Wikimedia Commons/Alexey Komarov, 31, Central Intelligence Agency, 11, Conkoch, 44, Rallison321, 30, Tom Patterson, 13, 김홍빈(산악인), 6

Every effort has been made to contact copyright holders for material reproduced in this book. Any omissions will be rectified in subsequent printings if notice is given to the publisher.

Copyright © 2025 Creative Education, Creative Paperbacks
International copyright reserved in all countries.
No part of this book may be reproduced in any form
without written permission from the publisher.

Library of Congress Cataloging-in-Publication Data
Names: Musolf, Hank, author.
Title: Mount Everest / Hank Musolf.
Description: Mankato, Minnesota : Creative Education and Creative Paperbacks, [2025] | Series: The seven summits | Includes bibliographical references and index. | Audience: Ages 10–14 | Audience: Grades 4–6 | Summary: "Mount Everest is Asia's–and the world's–tallest peak and a Seven Summits mountaineering challenge. This guide for kids age 12 and up examines the mountain's geologic and climbing history. Includes a glossary, sidebars, profiles of notable climbers, and further resources"—Provided by publisher.
Identifiers: LCCN 2024023453 (print) | LCCN 2024023454 (ebook) | ISBN 9798889892724 (library binding) | ISBN 9781682776384 (paperback) | ISBN 9798889893837 (ebook)
Subjects: LCSH: Everest, Mount (China and Nepal)—Juvenile literature.
Classification: LCC DS495.8.E9 M87 2025 (print) | LCC DS495.8.E9 (ebook) | DDC 954.96/1—dc23/eng/20240605
LC record available at https://lccn.loc.gov/2024023453
LC ebook record available at https://lccn.loc.gov/2024023454

Printed in the United States of America

His fingers lost to a previous mountaineering accident, Korean climber Kim Hong-bin celebrates summiting Everest in 2007.

CONTENTS

Introduction 8

Chapter 1: Foot by Foot 11

Chapter 2: Life in the Shadow 19

Chapter 3: To the Summit 27

Chapter 4: Notable Climbers 37

Stories of the Summit 44

Glossary 46

Selected Bibliography 47

Websites 47

Index 48

MOUNT EVEREST

INTRODUCTION

A team of climbers begins their ascent up a snowy incline. The sky is clear and blue. The landscape is desolate but beautiful. More and more, it's getting harder for the climbers to breathe. There is less oxygen the higher they climb, and they feel it in their lungs. The climbers face many dangers with each step, such as avalanches, rivers of ice, **crevasses**, and powerful subzero winds. The climb can be deadly. But despite the threats, the climbers continue. For mountaineers such as these, taking on this incredible challenge is worth the risks, because once they conquer it, they'll be standing on top of the world.

Mount Everest is the tallest mountain in Asia and the highest point on Earth. Part of the **Seven Summits**, Everest has fascinated and inspired people living in its shadow for thousands of years. Today, about 800 climbers from around the world attempt to reach its peak each year. Not everyone succeeds, but that doesn't stop countless others from trying.

A memorial shrine, decorated with Tibetan Buddhist prayer flags, rests in the shadow of Mount Everest.

Mountaineers use ladder bridges to cross deep cracks in the ice on the way to Everest's summit.

CHAPTER 1: FOOT BY FOOT

THE NATIONAL FLAG OF NEPAL

Everest. Aconcagua. Denali. Kilimanjaro. Elbrus. Vinson. Kosciuszko. These are the Seven Summits, the tallest mountains on each of the seven continents. Climber Richard Bass was the first to scale all seven mountains. His book documenting his travels, *Seven Summits*, helped to popularize the idea of climbing the tallest peaks. Bass described the motivation to climb all the mountains as a thrill of overcoming a huge challenge. He stated, "There has to be a spirit of adventure to it, and an element of uncertainty and risk." The last mountain Bass scaled on his major expedition was Mount Everest. Mount Everest is the world's tallest mountain above sea level. Measuring 29,032 feet (8,849 meters), it is the tallest of the Seven Summits by almost 2,000 feet (610 m). Mount Aconcagua is second tallest. Everest's summit is 5.5 miles (8.9 kilometers) above sea level. Although Everest is located in Nepal, its peak sits on the border between Nepal and Tibet. The mountain is part of the towering Great Himalayas. Many layers of rocks and minerals make up Everest, including garnet, gneiss, granite, limestone, and schist.

MOUNT EVEREST

According to **geologists**, Mount Everest's story began around 40 to 50 million years ago, when two huge rocky pieces of Earth's crust, called **tectonic plates**, smashed together. These plates were the Indian-Australian plate and the Eurasian plate. The collision caused the Indian-Australian plate to go underneath the Eurasian plate, which pushed the landmass upward. Around 25 to 30 million years ago, the Himalayan range, including Everest, began to rise. The plates continue to move to this day, and because of this, Everest's height continues to change. The mountain gradually grows taller as time passes. Each year, the mountain grows approximately 0.2 inch (5 millimeters).

While Mount Everest has been around for millions of years, and local people have lived in its shadow for thousands of years, the peak was not known by people outside the area until fairly recently. After its "discovery" by British **surveyors**, everyone wanted to be the first to measure the mountain's height. In 1802, William Lambton researched the Himalayan mountains, hoping to chart them for Great Britain. His proposal, called the Great **Trigonometrical** Survey, included measuring from the southernmost point in India all the way to the Himalayas. Lambton worked on this survey project until his death in 1823. His work carried on in the hands of his assistant, George Everest.

Continuing Lambton's work, Everest led an expedition across India, measuring and calculating miles of desert and jungle. His surveying was incredibly accurate. Surveying methods of today produce results that are only slightly more accurate than his calculations. Everest retired in 1843.

The Great Trigonometrical Survey group pressed on toward the Himalayas under the leadership of surveyor general Andrew Waugh. They referred to the

Monte Everest
Vista oeste-noroeste

BY ANY OTHER NAME

British surveyors to Everest in the 1800s called it "Gamma," followed by "peak b," as they guessed a nearby mountain, Kangchenjunga, was taller (thus, "peak a"). After that came "Peak XV," followed finally by "Mount Everest." The surveyors claimed not to know of any local names for the mountain. However, in the early 1900s, Swedish explorer Sven Hedin discovered a 1733 French map that showed Everest's name as Chomolunga, a Tibetan word. Today, other names for the mountain include Chajamlungma, Qomolangma, and Zhumulangma Peak. The Nepali Sagarmatha means "Goddess of the Sky."

MOUNT EVEREST

By today's standards, Tenzing Norgay [left] and Edmund Hillary climbed Everest in 1953 with primitive gear.

tallest mountain as Peak XV. In 1856, Waugh pitched naming the mountain after George Everest. This ignored the name the local Tibetans gave the mountain, Chomolungma, which roughly translates to "Goddess of the Mountain." They also ignored the Nepali name, Sagarmatha, which means "Goddess of the Sky." Waugh claimed to not have been able to find any local name for the mountain. Everest resisted naming the mountain after himself, as he tended to use local words for naming places. Plus, it's likely he had never even laid eyes on the giant mountain. Still, Waugh persisted and named the peak Mount Everest.

Records indicate that mathematician Radhanath Sikdar was likely the first person to calculate Mount Everest's true height. Hired by the Great Trigonometrical Survey at age 19, Sikdar eventually became the team's

MOUNT EVEREST

"Chief Computer." He used triangulation, a geometric process that determines an unknown point's location by using telescope-like instruments called theodolites. With theodolites, the team was able to calculate the height of the peak from their base camp below the mountain. They first recorded two locations on the ground, A and B, and measured the distance between them. Then, they went to location A, pointed the theodolite to the mountain peak, and took a reading. They did the same thing from location B, creating a triangle. Using the known distance and the angle measurements, Sikdar was able to determine Everest's height.

Researching Everest in the early 1900s, before modern technology existed, was slow, cold work.

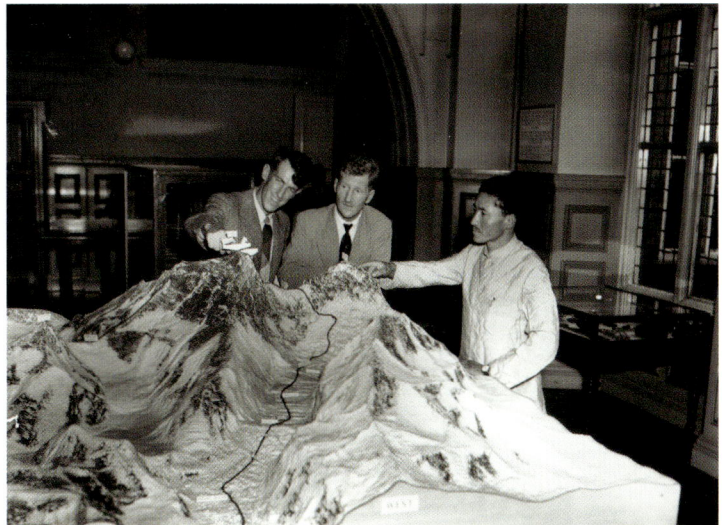

A large-scale model of Mount Everest showed the route taken by the first summiteeers in 1953.

At the time, Sikdar was considered by many, including George Everest, to be one of the best mathematicians in the world. His work lived up to that statement. Sikdar measured Mount Everest to be exactly 29,000 feet (8,839 m). Waugh added 2 feet (0.6 m) to that number when he announced the official height as 29,002 feet (8,840 m) in 1856. He figured his number would come under less scrutiny and not appear to be a number rounded up or down.

Further surveys have been done by various countries since then. In 1954, almost 100 years after the Great Trigonometrical Survey, the Survey of India measured Everest using many of the same methods. Their measurement was 29,028 feet (8,848 m). Some of the surveys done from the 1970s to the 1980s yielded questionable results. A 1992 survey by Italy utilized **global positioning system** technology to measure the mountain. Their measurement was 29,023 feet (8,846 m). A 1999 survey by the United States gave a close measurement at 29,035 feet (8,850 m). A 2005 survey by China measured the mountain at 29,017 feet (8,844 m). The surveys from 1954, 1999, and 2005 are still recognized today and used by various groups and organizations. In 2020, China and Nepal announced an official height for Mount Everest at 29,032 feet (8,849 m), based on surveys the two countries had measured in 2019 and 2020.

Like Everest, Ama Dablam, part of the eastern Himalayan range, is permanently snow-capped.

CHAPTER 2: LIFE IN THE SHADOW

The climate on Mount Everest's peak is harsh. On average, the warmest temperature in summer is around -2 degrees Fahrenheit (-19 degrees Celsius), and the coldest temperature in winter is around -33 °F (-36 °C). The weather changes rapidly but remains freezing cold. Frostbite is an ever-present danger for climbers. And Everest's winds are some of the strongest on Earth, with hurricane-force winds battering the summit more than 50 percent of the time.

Above 20,000 feet (6,096 m), snow is permanent on Everest, which means no vegetation grows on the peak. Although a few kinds of life have been observed in higher elevations, such as Himalayan jumping spiders and a couple bird species, almost all wildlife is confined to areas around the mountain's base.

The base of Everest is home to a beautiful natural landscape. A forested area contains mainly Himalayan birch, fir, juniper, oak, and pine trees. Bright pink flowers called rhododendrons are common in the lower area of Everest. These are Nepal's national flower. White flowers with fuzzy petals called edelweiss

MOUNT EVEREST

YETI

can also be found in this region. A wide variety of animals live in these forests. There are more than 850 species of birds in Nepal, including Himalayan monal, great rosefinches, vultures, and golden eagles. Plenty of mammals can be seen around the base, though many are rare. Musk deer roam, while Himalayan black bears search for food. Red pandas live in trees and eat bamboo. Pikas are small mammals that live in rocky landscapes. Snow leopards make their home in the higher altitudes of the region. They are incredibly shy, and their light fur color allows them to hide easily in the snow.

Due to the same factors that keep plants and animals from living on Everest, no groups of people live on the mountain, either. Instead, the communities nearest to Everest are in the valleys below it. Studies of ancient remains in the area suggest the earliest people in the area migrated from East Asia. Most of the population of the valleys are Sherpa. The Sherpas are an ethnic group of Tibetans who migrated from Tibet to Nepal around the 15th century. Many Sherpas live in Khumbu Valley, the entryway for people wanting to climb Mount Everest. The word *Sherpa* originally meant "easterner." Today, the word is used as a catch-all description for the guides who assist climbers. Sherpas know the best routes up the slopes. Without them, many climbers would be completely lost.

The Sherpa people weren't always mountaineers, however. Because they were Nyingm Buddhists, Sherpas revered the Himalayas as the home of gods. Traditions and customs discouraged exploration of the holy mountains. The Sherpa people also had no equipment to help them climb to the higher peaks. They made their living by farming, raising cattle, and working with fabrics. It wasn't until the 1920s, when visiting explorers from Great Britain sought their assistance, that the

YETI'S HOME

One of the world's best-known mythological creatures has ties to Mount Everest: the yeti. A figure from Nepalese folklore, the yeti appears in tales as a frightening beast, one created, perhaps, to inspire children not to stray too far from home. In 1951, British explorer Eric Shipton found a massive footprint while climbing Mount Everest. He took a picture of it that was later published in a magazine, sparking rumors that a yeti lived on the mountain. Through the years, numerous searches have been made, but none has found the elusive abominable snowman.

MOUNTAIN FISH

The preserved remains of ancient fish bones have been found on Mount Everest! So have seashells. Although the discoveries sound fake, they are the real result of plate tectonics. Millions of years ago, Everest was on the ocean floor. As plates shifted, collided, and rose, sea life preserved in limestone was brought upward. The taller the mountain grew, the farther up the ocean remains were carried. The prehistoric Tethys Sea, from which Everest rose, was home to marine animals and plants whose remains are preserved deep in the mountain's rocks.

Sherpa people earned their reputation as expert guides. They impressed the British with their hard work and incredible strength when scaling Everest.

Sherpas are naturals at mountaineering. Some people use the word *superhuman* to define their climbing skills. Researchers have conducted studies to try to understand how Sherpas can ascend Everest so efficiently. One reason for the efficiency is the ability to handle oxygen. The Sherpa people have lived at such high altitudes for so long, even in the valleys below the Himalayan mountains, that their bodies have adapted to the low-oxygen conditions. Climbers from outside the region often face **altitude sickness** from making the ascent. They experience severe headaches and other symptoms that can slow down or completely stop their climbs.

In 1953, Sherpa mountaineer Tenzing Norgay was one of the first people to climb to Mount Everest's peak. He reached the summit with another explorer, New Zealander Edmund Hillary. Norgay was once quoted as saying, "You cannot be a good mountaineer, however great your ability, unless you are cheerful and have the spirit of comradeship. Friends are as important as achievement." News of the successful climb spread quickly around the world, just as Nepal opened its borders to more tourism. Life for the Sherpa people changed significantly. More and more tourists arrived, all wanting to try to climb Mount Everest and to hire Sherpas to guide them. The Sherpa people went from being a quiet, closed off community to one that was heavily tied to tourist mountaineering.

Countless Everest climbing groups have owed their success to skilled Sherpa guides.

Sherpas are often the unsung heroes of Everest climbs. They regularly bear the weight of expeditions—not only the physical loads but also responsibility for climbers' safety. They carry oxygen tanks and other heavy loads and take greater risks as they assist others. Despite the dangers, Sherpa guides historically have been overlooked and underpaid, receiving significantly less than other guides.

In the 1950s and again in the 1970s, Sherpa guides protested their harsh conditions and poor equipment. Normally, when a climber reaches the peak of Everest, Nepal's Department of Tourism presents the climber with a completion certificate. In 2016, the department was accused of not giving 300 Sherpa climbers their certificates. About one-third of all deaths on Mount Everest have been Sherpa. In 2014, 16 Sherpas died traversing the extremely dangerous Khumbu Icefall. The Sherpa people demanded greater safety measures for guides and better training for climbers. Since then, as a positive step, helicopters have been used more often for rescues. Previously the burden would fall on Sherpa guides to get injured or sick people to safer locations.

In recent years, the number of Sherpa who choose to enter the climbing profession has decreased. Many Sherpa people are choosing safer job paths. One factor that affects all guides and climbers is climate change. Mount Everest has been feeling its effects. With rising temperatures, many locations on the mountain are changing. Icy spots are now rockier. Avalanches and landslides are happening more often. Floods and droughts affect the area farmlands, as well. Work is being done to adapt to the changing climate, but the dangers and risks are still present for everyone who lives near or visits Everest.

Slippery, near-vertical climbs require mental focus and tools such as ice axes for balance and support.

CHAPTER 3: TO THE SUMMIT

Summiting Mount Everest is an incredible feat. It takes great strength, endurance, and mental focus. To prepare for the challenge, a climber must train. One's body and mind must be in peak condition. The proper gear and equipment are also vital. Without the right skills, tools, and training, a climber risks injury—or worse—and may put fellow climbers in danger, too.

Physical training is key for anyone attempting to climb Everest. But an average gym workout isn't necessarily going to be enough. Instead, climbers are urged to do special mountaineering workouts that prepare the body for the specific obstacles they will face on the mountain. Climbers need to be able to scale all sorts of terrain on Everest while carrying as much as 60 pounds (27 kilograms) of gear and other supplies. Training plans should focus on building leg strength, **cardiovascular** strength, and overall physical endurance. It is also

MOUNT EVEREST

important to train at higher altitudes. Climbers must be able to handle the thinner oxygen at Everest's peak. Training for at least a year is recommended.

A climber must have the right clothing for their journey up Mount Everest. Multiple pairs of boots and shoes are required, including climbing boots, light hiking shoes for dry trails, and **insulated** booties for sleeping. Multiple pairs of heavyweight and lightweight socks are a must-have, too. Thick gloves, mittens, well-insulated and waterproof jackets and pants, wool-blend base layers, facemasks, hats, and a helmet help keep climbers comfortable and safe in the freezing Everest conditions. Glacier goggles are also recommended. They protect climbers' eyes by blocking out bright sunlight reflected off snow. Hand and toe warmers made of natural ingredients that warm up when exposed to oxygen can make a major difference in the bitter cold.

The proper gear and equipment are important for climbers. Although lists may vary, mountaineers usually bring backpacks, food, water bottles, a camping cook set, and a stove. They also bring a heavily insulated sleeping bag, sleeping pad, and tent.

Climbers should prepare for all kinds of terrain, bringing equipment that will keep them safe in snowy, icy, and rocky conditions. Common equipment includes harnesses, **crampons**, climbing poles, ice axes, and an altitude watch. Harnesses are a set of belts and straps that are connected to ropes. They make climbing easier and keep climbers secure if they fall. Crampons are spikes that attach to boots. They help with traction in snowy and icy terrain. Similarly, climbing poles help keep a person upright in the snow. They look like ski poles but are much sturdier. Ice axes also help with stability, especially on icy obstacles such as frozen waterfalls. They have a straight shaft with a sharp pick on one end

In his 2008 PBS film, mountaineer David Breashears tells the story of eight climbers who died in a blizzard on Everest in 1996.

MOUNT EVEREST

and a hammer on the other. An altitude watch helps climbers monitor changes in pressure and predict weather changes.

In addition to bringing gear and equipment, climbers are also required to have a permit to climb Everest. In 2023, a permit cost $11,000. A travel visa for longer than a month is required, too, as are costs for hotels and flights.

The recommended time to visit Mount Everest is May. The weather is at its best for climbing purposes. Eighty percent of Everest climbs have happened between May 15 and May 27. But climbs have been made year-round. Fall is the next best time. Whenever a mountaineer visits, plans need to be made far in advance. Climbers expecting to ascend in May usually arrive in Nepal months prior to get used to the higher elevation.

With all the travel plans, gear, equipment, clothing, and training set, the next step is making the climb. Most climbers take one of two routes up Everest:

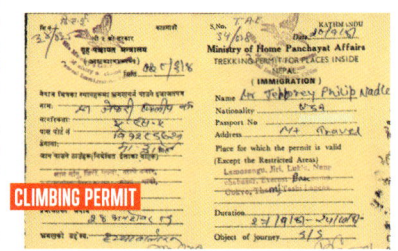

the North Col or the South Col. There are other ways up the mountain, but they are incredibly dangerous and generally avoided. For a time, the northern route was cheaper and was favored partially for that reason. In recent years, however, prices for the two routes have evened out, and the south route has been more commonly traveled. Each route has its pros and cons. The southern route is steeper. This can potentially mean more difficult climbing. Helicopter rescues are only possible on the southern route. The northern route is less crowded. It doesn't require a walking trek to base camp, but climbers can face worse weather conditions.

Kathmandu is Nepal's largest city, with an estimated population of 1.4 million.

The South Col, or Southeast Ridge route, starts in the capital city of Kathmandu, Nepal. Mountaineers fly from there to Khumbu Valley. A trek across the valley showcases beautiful sites of the region on the way to base camp. Everest Base Camp is located in Sagarmatha National Park. Tens of thousands of tourists visit the park each year, although only about 800 set out to climb the mountain. Once climbers reach base camp, they must spend a few weeks there to further **acclimatize**. The most dangerous part of the southern route, the Khumbu Icefall, lies on the way to the first camp.

The Khumbu Icefall is a section of the Khumbu Glacier. Essentially, it is a river of ice that shifts. Climbers face numerous risks when hiking it, including avalanches, collapsing ice, and crevasses. After passing the icefall, the next challenge for climbers on the southern route is avoiding avalanches on the way to the second camp. The major obstacle en route to the third camp is climbing the Lhotse

CHAPTER 3: TO THE SUMMIT

KHUMBU ICEFALL

The Khumbu Icefall is one of the most dangerous sections on Everest. It is relatively early in the climb, at 17,300 feet (5,273 m). Because the glacier is constantly moving, crevasses can open beneath climbers at any time. Staying attached to a rope is the best way for climbers to stay safe. Other threats include collapsing structures of ice and rock. A speedy but safe trip over the icefall is recommended. Climbers are also advised to stay off the icefall when the sun's rays are touching it, as that increases the risk of sudden shifts and movement.

Face. Lhotse is a mountain in the Himalayas, and a section of it must be climbed with a rope to complete the southern route to Everest's summit. Falling rocks and ice are common dangers.

After the third camp, the next leg of the journey passes through the Yellow Band, a stretch of sandstone rocks, and the Geneva Spur, another rocky landscape. After braving that, mountaineers reach the South Col itself, a flat area where incredibly strong winds batter those who dare step foot on it.

Pushing toward the summit, climbers first take a small rest on a ledge called "The Balcony," which offers stunning views of the peaks. Then it's a series of rocky steps and a trudge through deep snow. Following a dangerous trek across a knife-edge ridge, climbers reach the Hillary Step, a rock wall that must be ascended with rope. After that, it's the final push to the summit.

The North Col, or Northeast Ridge route, begins in Tibet. The northern route is shorter than the southern route, but much harsher weather must be faced. Most of the route is at a higher altitude, too, and if climbers need to spend more time in those high altitudes due to storms, altitude sickness can occur. A major benefit to the northern route is the lack of icefall.

To start this route, mountaineers usually travel by vehicle to the Rongbuk Monastery, where the base camp is set up. The Tibetan Buddhist monastery is the highest monastery in the world, at 16,500 feet (5,029 m). From here, explorers are on their own. There is no outside help from helicopters or other

MOUNT EVEREST

emergency vehicles past this point. Climbers then head to an interim camp and an advanced base camp, where they acclimatize to the area's altitude.

To reach the North Col, climbers hold on to a rope that's thousands of feet long. The rope is connected to the North Col itself. Climbers can use an **ascender** here. Crampons are necessary for maintaining footing on the icy ground. The next few camps are past this steep climb, and from there, teams begin their expedition to the summit.

Another section of rope-holding follows, then a trip through the Yellow Band. After that, climbers see various rock structures. The Three Steps are difficult climbs, requiring proper footing and focus. Mushroom Rock is used as a waypoint marker of sorts to let climbers know how far they are up the mountain. The last hurdle on the northern route is the Summit Pyramid, a snowy slope that leaves climbers exposed to intense weather. Once a mountaineer is past that, a hike of 500 feet (152 m) brings them to the summit.

Whichever route a climber takes, the view from Everest's summit is incredible. Reaching the summit has been described as life changing. One may feel as though they can genuinely touch the deep blue sky above them. The Himalayan mountains stretch out all around. People who have reached the summit report that the sense of accomplishment is like nothing else in the world.

CHOPPER RESCUE

Helicopter rescues on Everest are becoming more common. They require precision and teamwork from everyone involved. Pilots must brave bad weather and locales with no easy landing spaces. During a long-line rescue, a rescuer is lowered by rope from a helicopter down to the person in need. The person is secured to the rescuer, and the helicopter lifts up, its cargo dangling below, flying until the pilot can reach a safe place to land. Once the helicopter touches down, the rescuer assesses the person and then takes them to the nearest hospital. People may need rescue for injuries or afflictions such as altitude sickness or frostbite.

CHAPTER 3: TO THE SUMMIT

British mountaineer George Mallory (1886–1924) was known for his confident, catlike climbing ability.

CHAPTER 4: NOTABLE CLIMBERS

owling winds blow over the tents of a team climbing Mount Everest. The wind gusts are so strong that they've knocked down the tents multiple times. The explorers can't even call out to each other because the wind drowns out their voices. Shivering in the frigid air, the climbers can only dig in and wait until the winds die down. Only then can they truly rest. In facing dangers such as this, explorers may find themselves asking why they've taken on this challenge. Why *do* so many people want to climb Everest? Why do they risk their lives to try to conquer the icy mountain?

After Edmund Hillary and Tenzing Norgay's successful climb in 1953, traveling to the top of Mount Everest became a major goal for many climbers around the world. Some of the most notable and record-breaking climbers etched their name in history with their ascents.

Before Hillary and Norgay completed their climb, George Mallory was among those who paved the way for them. Mallory was part of various

MOUNT EVEREST

Climber Junko Tabei posed with the national flags of Nepal and Japan atop Mount Everest in 1975.

expeditions to explore Mount Everest, joining the British survey team in the 1920s. In 1924, Mallory attempted to reach the top alongside fellow explorer Sandy Irvine. When asked why so many people felt so moved to reach the summit, Mallory answered simply, "Because it's there." Sadly, Mallory and Irvine died on the expedition, and their bodies went missing. For decades, their fate was a mystery. Years later, some climbers set out to find Mallory's body, and it was eventually located in 1999. It is unknown if Mallory reached the top of the mountain during his climb. In 2019, climber Mark Synnott attempted to find Irvine's body. He hoped to find the camera the duo had brought with them almost a century prior. His attempt was unsuccessful.

Junko Tabei was born in Japan in 1939. Her love for hiking and mountaineering began around age 10. In 1975, Tabei became the first woman to reach Mount Everest's summit. It was a memorable trek for many reasons. Halfway through her expedition,

LOTS OF LITTER

An unfortunate side effect of so many climbers ascending Everest is the amount of trash littering the mountain. The average climber leaves behind 18 pounds (8 kg) of trash and waste per visit, and most of it stays on the mountain. This potentially brings many risks. The sheer amount of garbage could affect water sources in the valley below as runoff trickles off the mountain. Between 2019 and 2023, a cleanup campaign collected 110 tons (100 metric tons) of trash from Everest. In 2024, climbers were required to use government-issued "poop bags" to bring their own waste off the mountain.

Clean-up crews collect trash left by climbers from Everest's slopes.

she and her team were struck by an avalanche. Tabei was bruised and injured, as were the rest of the team members, but she carried on until she reached the peak. In 1992, she became the first woman to complete the Seven Summits. By the time she died in 2016, she had climbed more than 70 of the world's tallest peaks.

Lhakpa Sherpa has set multiple records on Mount Everest. In 2000, she became the first Nepalese woman to reach the summit. That wasn't her only trip to the top, however. She made the journey 9 more times as of 2022, bringing her total to 10. This is the most Everest summits of any woman in history. Speaking about her climbing triumphs and her status as an inspirational figure for people around the world, Sherpa said, "I felt like I'd changed Sherpa culture, the status of Sherpa women, and Nepalese women. I enjoyed being outside of my home, and I wanted to share that feeling with all women." She added, "I've had a challenging life. Mountains made me happy and relaxed. I will never give up. I want young women not to give up."

The record holder for youngest person ever to reach Mount Everest's summit is Jordan Romero. He was 13 years old when he reached the top of the mountain in 2010. In 2011, he completed the Seven Summits. Romero's climbs met some

MOUNT EVEREST

criticism, due to concerns about facing such high risks at such a young age. His record will likely remain unbroken. Tibet has raised the age for permits to 16 since Romero's climb.

Arumina Sinha faced some of the greatest challenges in her summit of Mount Everest. In 2011, a tragic assault resulted in injuries that forced Sinha to have one of her legs amputated. While recovering in the hospital, Sinha vowed that she would one day climb Everest. Two years later, in 2013, she did just that. She completed the grueling task, becoming the first female amputee to reach Everest's peak. It was an inspiring accomplishment that ranks with some of the greatest climbs in Everest history.

Since Hillary and Norgay's climb in 1953, more than 6,600 people have summited Mount Everest (as of January 2024). Some have left behind mementos for future climbers to find. Photos of family members and colorful Tibetan prayer flags are often placed on the mountain, memorializing and leaving messages of hope at the highest point on Earth. A handful of climbers have left behind so much more, their bodies still lost and frozen on Everest's slopes.

It may be harrowing, dangerous, and potentially deadly to reach the summit of Mount Everest. The way down can be just as difficult, if not more so, than the way up. But for climbers with a passion for adventure, it's hard to pass up the chance to scale Everest and celebrate at the top of the world.

BURIED BODIES

No one knows the exact number of bodies that lie frozen on Mount Everest. More than 300 people have died on the mountain, and it is estimated that about 200 bodies are still buried in the snow and ice. Because of the freezing conditions, the bodies are nearly impossible to recover. Many of the deaths were due to accidents or altitude sickness. The deadliest year in Everest's recorded history was 2015, when a single avalanche killed 19 climbers. Tracking chips were handed out to climbers for the first time in 2024 to help with search and rescue efforts in case of emergency.

MOUNT EVEREST

STORIES OF THE SUMMIT

ERIK WEIHENMAYER

All Mount Everest climbs are inspiring to some degree, but Erik Weihenmayer's is especially so. In 2001, Erik became the first person with blindness to reach Everest's summit.

Erik was born in Princeton, New Jersey, in 1968. He lost his eyesight at age 13 due to a condition called retinoschisis, which causes the eye's retina to gradually decline. He wanted to continue playing sports, so he took up wrestling. He also discovered rock wall climbing, which ignited a lifelong passion for the sport. Some of Erik's friends said it would be impossible for him to take up outdoor climbing. But Erik was drawn to mountaineering and spent much of his free time climbing as a hobby.

After earning a teaching degree at Lesley University in Massachusetts, Erik joined a mountain climbing club. He climbed several mountain peaks, eventually conquering Mount Denali and Mount Kilimanjaro. He set his sights on Everest next. Getting to the mountain proved difficult, however, as many Sherpa guides did not want to take the risk of protecting a blind climber. But when Erik arrived in Nepal in 2001, he proved he was up to the challenge. He made the climb and reached the top of the tallest peak in the world. By 2008, Erik had reached the peaks of all the Seven Summits. Today, he works for an organization he founded called No Barriers, which seeks to help those with stories like his.

LUCY WESTLAKE

Lucy Westlake holds the distinction of being the youngest American woman to climb Mount Everest. Born in 2003, Lucy began mountaineering when she was seven years old. After she enjoyed her first mountain climb, her family learned about high pointing, a challenge to reach every tallest point in a certain area. For

Lucy, that challenge meant climbing to the highest point in each of the 50 U.S. states. By age 13, she'd completed all but one: Alaska's Mount Denali. Climbing it proved too difficult for her first attempt, but Lucy didn't quit. She tried again at age 17, and that time, she succeeded.

After completing the U.S. high points, Lucy set her sights on the rest of the Seven Summits. In 2022, she tackled Everest. She said that while Denali was the most difficult climb physically, Everest was the most difficult climb emotionally. Her ascent was powered by gummy bears, Oreos, and ramen. She said sugar kept her going.

Lucy faced hardships on her climb, as it was the first one without her father by her side. She described the Himalayas as the most beautiful mountains she'd ever seen. "You have this beautiful mix of green lush mountains that go into these beautiful white peaks. The mix of ecosystems up there is just beautiful." Lucy hopes to complete the rest of the Seven Summits by the time she's 20 years old.

MOUNT EVEREST

GLOSSARY

acclimatize—to adjust or get used to a new environment

altitude sickness—swelling of the lungs or brain caused by air pressure at high altitudes

ascender—a handle or grip that attaches to a rope or fixed line and allows the user to pull themselves upward

cardiovascular—having to do with the heart

crampon—a metal plate with spikes attached to a boot for walking or climbing on rock or ice

crevasse—a deep crack in a glacier or other body of ice

geologist—a scientist who studies the history of Earth, particularly by examining rocks

global positioning system—GPS; a system of satellites, computers, and other electronic devices that work together to determine the location of objects or living things that carry a trackable device

insulated—protected from the loss of heat

monastery—a building or buildings housing a community of people who've taken religious vows, especially monks

Seven Summits—a group that includes the tallest mountain on each of the seven continents

surveyor—a person who measures (surveys) or estimates the dimensions of land

tectonic plate—a huge, rocky piece of Earth's shell that slowly moves around the world, carrying the continents and the ocean floor with it

trigonometrical—having to do with the properties of triangles and the branch of mathematics called trigonometry

SELECTED BIBLIOGRAPHY

Bell, Steve, ed. *Seven Summits: The Quest to Reach the Highest Point on Every Continent.* Boston: Little, Brown, 2000.

Calamur, Krishnadev. "Who Are Nepal's Sherpas?" NPR. April 22, 2014. https://www.npr.org/sections/parallels/2014/04/22/305954983/who-are-nepals-sherpas.

Conefrey, Mick. *Everest 1922: The Epic Story of the First Attempt on the World's Highest Mountain.* New York: Pegasus Books, 2022.

Hernandez, Joe. "Read the Last Letters of George Mallory, Who Died Climbing Mount Everest in 1924." NPR. April 23, 2024. https://www.npr.org/2024/04/23/1246625840/george-mallory-everest-explorer-letters-cambridge.

Synnott, Mark. *The Third Pole: Mystery, Obsession, and Death on Mount Everest.* New York: Dutton, 2021.

Venables, Stephen, Wilfrid Noyce, (Henry Cecil) John Hunt, et al. "Mount Everest." *Encyclopedia Britannica.* July 27, 2024. https://www.britannica.com/place/Mount-Everest.

Viesturs, Ed, and David Roberts. *No Shortcuts to the Top: Climbing the World's 14 Highest Peaks.* New York: Broadway Books, 2006.

WEBSITES

7 Summits Club
https://7summitsclub.com
Learn about the world's tallest peaks and the people who climb them.

Britannica Kids
https://kids.britannica.com/students/article/Mount-Everest/274233
Discover facts about Mount Everest's physical features and climbers.

Everest
https://ntb.gov.np/everest
Explore the Nepal Tourism Board's official website for Mount Everest.

MOUNT EVEREST

INDEX

Aconcagua, Mount, 1, 11
altitude sickness, 23, 35, 43
ancient fish, 22
Bass, Richard, 11
climate change effects, 25
climbing
  certificates, 25
  equipment, 10, 20, 25, 26, 27, 28, 30
  gear, 14, 25, 26, 27, 28, 30, 34
  permits, 30
  rescues, 25, 30, 35
  season, 30
  supplies, 27
  training, 25, 27–28, 30
Denali (McKinley), Mount, 1, 11, 44, 45
Elbrus, Mount, 1, 11
Everest, George, 12, 14, 17
Everest, Mount
  deaths, 25, 29, 38, 42, 43
  European discovery, 12
  first summiteers, 17, 23
  first woman summiteer, 38
  formation, 12
  height, 1, 11, 12, 14, 16, 17
  location, 1, 8, 11
  name origins, 13, 14
  number of summiteers, 8, 42
  trash, 40, 41
  youngest summiteer, 41–42
Great Trigonometrical Survey, 12, 14, 17
Hillary, Edmund, 14, 23, 37, 42
Himalayas, 11, 12, 18, 20, 23, 33, 34, 45
Hong-bin, Kim, 6
Irvine, Sandy, 38
Kathmandu, Nepal, 31
Khumbu Glacier, 31, 32
Khumbu Icefall, 25, 31, 32

Khumbu Valley, 20, 31
Kilimanjaro, Mount, 1, 11, 44
Kosciuszko, Mount, 1, 11
Lambton, William, 12
Lhotse, 31, 33
Mallory, George, 36, 37–38
Norgay, Tenzing, 14, 23, 37, 42
PBS film, 29
rock types, 11
Romero, Jordan, 41–42
Rongbuk Monastery, 33
routes
  North Col, 30, 33, 34
  South Col, 30, 31, 33
Sagarmatha National Park, 31
Seven Summits, 1, 8, 41, 45
Sherpa, Lhakpa, 41
Sherpa people, 20, 23, 25, 41, 44
Shipton, Eric, 21
Sikdar, Radhanath, 14, 16, 17
Sinha, Arumina, 42
Tabei, Junko, 38, 41
tectonic plates, 12, 22
temperatures, 19, 25
vegetation, 19, 20
Vinson, Mount, 1, 11
Waugh, Andrew, 12, 14, 17
Weihenmayer, Erik, 44
Westlake, Lucy, 45
wildlife, 19, 20
winds, 8, 19, 33, 37
Yellow Band, 33, 34
Yeti, 20, 21